President Trump

By Tom Connor & Jim Downey

GRAND CENTRAL
PUBLISHING

New York Boston

Grand Central Publishing
Hachette Book Group
1290 Avenue of the Americas
New York, NY 10104
grandcentralpublishing.com
twitter.com/grandcentralpub

First Edition: June 2016

Grand Central Publishing is a division of Hachette Book Group, Inc.

The Grand Central Publishing name and logo are trademarks of Hachette Book Group, Inc.

The publisher is not responsible for websites (or their content) that are not owned by the publisher.

The Hachette Speakers Bureau provides a wide range of authors for speaking events. To find out more, go to www.hachettespeakersbureau.com or call (866) 376-6591.

ISBNs: 978-1-4555-7009-6 (trade paperback), 978-1-4555-7034-8 (ebook)

Printed in the United States of America

Book designed by Laura Campbell, campbell + company

WOR

10 9 8 7 6 5 4 3 2 1

TRUMP TIME

VOL I, NO. 1, | 2016

Cover Story

Elected! Donald K. Trump

Donald K. Trump's road to the White House was paved with open-minded, freedom-loving Americans from all across the country.

by Donald K. Trump 32

Constitutional Amendments

With less and less time to read in today's mobile society, the President exercises his right to edit out some pesky and unnecessary language.

by Donald K. Trump 8

Immigration, for Some

The President's plan to solve one of the most sensitive issues of our times was inspired by his interpretation of an American anthem: "This land is *my* land, this land ain't *your* land!"

by Donald K. Trump 60

On the cover: Long before the Republican Convention, Donald K. Trump jumped the White House fence to photobomb himself in front of what he knew would be his future residence.

Credit: AP Photo/John Locher

◀ *Get Behind Trump team members, page 32*

An issue unlike any other.

IN THIS ISSUE, READERS WILL FIND LITTLE IF ANYTHING of what they have come to expect from one of the most respected publications in the history of American journalism. For this failure to deliver unbiased news coverage, we feel we must take some measure of responsibility. Earlier this year, under pressure from a majority shareholder, we foolishly and prematurely approved a cover story trumpeting the historic win of a then-candidate in the Republican race for the White House. That the shareholder and the candidate were one and the same augured ill not just for this magazine but for all publications that find themselves at the mercy of deep pockets in opportunistic pants. Yet ever since our parent, Time Warner, decided to spin off its printed-material children two years ago, we have been prey to the whims of mercenary foster parents who could use and abuse us at will for their own narcissistic ends. Today, as editors and reporters for *TrumpTIME*, we have as little say over its contents as orphan children have over their fates. So be it. We want to take this opportunity to personally thank you, dear readers, for your patience and loyalty as our pages have shrunk to the size of parody magazines and our focus has narrowed sharply and dangerously. Please do not worry about us. By the time the newly elected President takes office, we should be in Canada, along with many other Americans, where we hope to find work again as the editor of a legitimate, independent magazine, the kind where one needn't wash one's hands thoroughly and repeatedly after publishing each issue. May God keep you and our once-great nation safe as we enter the End Times.

—*Names & photos withheld pending future employment*

Letter from the Commander/Editor-in-Chief

A Presidency like no other.

I'M A HUGE BELIEVER IN THE FIRST AMENDMENT: Any American should be free to say whatever he wants whenever he wants to, no matter who he might be making fun of (just ask the losers in the Republican debates!) But I also happen to be a very, very successful businessman. These two passions of mine nicely coincide in this issue of the magazine, in which I bought a 51-percent stake following Time Warner's decision to spin off Time, Inc. two years ago. In the mutual interests, then, of unfettered capitalism and preserving our freedom of speech (more or less; see "Constitutional Edits and General Improvements" on page 8), I've exercised both my controlling shareholder and executive powers to take on the duties of writing and editing the better part of this debut issue of *TrumpTIME*. (By the way, I happen to be a very, very good writer. Have you bought my books? Well, you should. They're very, very good, as well as very, very successful; see also "review" on page 63.) In the following pages, readers will get a priceless preview of what promises to be the most amazing presidency in the history of the world, along with my thoughts on a broad range of many of the most pressing issues and executive decisions of the times. I believe you'll be as impressed with me as I am!

President-Elect Donald K. Trump

My Fellow Americans:

FIRST OF ALL, LET ME ASSERT MY FIRM BELIEF THAT THE ONLY THING WE HAVE TO FEAR IS FEAR ITSELF—nameless, sneaky, unreasoning, unjustified terror which paralyzes needed efforts to convert retreat into advance so we can win, win, win! So, with malice toward none, with charity for as many as we can afford, with firmness in the right as God gives us to see the right, and not be swayed by the gays, liberals and commies, let us strive on to finish the work we are in and get this deal done very, very successfully. We will bind up the nation's wounds and take care of everybody in the battle, their widow, even those poor suckers in Obamacare, and do everything we can possibly do to achieve and cherish a just and lasting peace among ourselves and with the smart nations who want to do it with us or pay the consequences. We are not enemies, and we wanna be friends with everybody, OK? So, though passion may have strained, it must not break our bonds of affection or any ongoing business deals. The mystic chords of memory, stretching very, very far, from every disaster on the battlefield and patriot grave to every living heart, hearthstone or any other oven all over this broad land, will yet swell the chorus of the Union singing that Fleetwood Mac song, "Don't Stop!" Never before have men or anybody with balls, really, tried so vast and formidable an experiment as that of administering the affairs of a continent under the form of a really, really great business. Upon the success of our experiment much depends, not only as regards our own welfare, social security and stock prices, but as regards the welfare of mankind and everybody. And so, my fellow Americans: Ask not what your country can do for you—ask what you can do for your President.

Constitutional edits and general improvements.

by Donald K. Trump

Me, the president of the United States, in Order to form ~~a more perfect Union~~ *a way better deal,* ~~establish Justice~~ *send loser nations to their rooms,* insure domestic Tranquility *(I got this down now, three time's a charm)*, provide for the common defense *(grow a pair!)*, promote the general Welfare *(how do you promote a General, he's the big cheese already, right?)* and secure the Blessings of Liberty to ourselves and our Posterity *(let's face it people, it's all our asses),* do ~~Ordain~~ *Order! (can we use real fucking English please?!)* and establish this Constitution for the United States of America.

Amendment I

Congress shall make no law *(yet)* respecting an establishment of religion *(minus mosques and possibly sinagogs—we'll see),* or prohibiting the free exercise or abridging the freedom of speech, or of the press *(whoa nelly!),* or the right of the people peaceably to assemble, and to petition the Government for a ~~redress~~ *(again with the fairy language!) new bunch* of grievances.

Amendment II

A well-regulated militia *(probably, except those whack jobs in Maine, Michigan or any of those hillbilly states that make moonshine)* being necessary to the security of a free state, the right of the people to keep and bear arms shall not be infringed.

Amendment III

No soldier shall, in time of peace be quartered in any house *or any of my hotels or resorts* without the consent of the owner, nor in time of war, but in a manner to be prescribed by ~~law~~ *Me.*

Amendment IV

The right of ~~the people~~ *most of the people (excluding writers for the Daily News and Vanity Fair or Perez Hilton)* to be secure in their persons, houses, *beach/vacation houses,* papers, *magazines,* and effects, against unreasonable searches and seizures, shall not be violated, *kissed or even touched (No means no!)* and no warrants shall issue, but upon probable *(my call)* cause, supported by oath or affirmation, and particularly describing the place to be searched, and the persons or things to be seized.

Amendment V

No person shall be held to answer for a capital, or otherwise infamous *(I always get this wrong. Infamous means famous, right?)* crime, unless on a ~~presentment~~ *(another one of these history words!)* conference call or the indictment of a grand jury, except in cases arising in the land or naval forces, *or Air Force, Astronauts or SWAT guys* or in the militia, when in actual service in time of war or public danger; nor shall any person be subject for the same offense to be twice put in jeopardy *(or any other game show, talk show or mini-series)* of life or limb; nor shall be compelled in any criminal case to be a witness against himself *(again, my call on this one)* nor be deprived of life, liberty, or property, without due process of law; nor shall private property be taken for public use, without just compensation.

Amendment VI

In all criminal prosecutions, the accused shall enjoy *(??? What mob guy enjoys his trial?)* the right to a speedy and public trial, by an impartial jury of the state and district *and neighborhood* wherein the crime shall have been committed, which district shall have been previously ascertained by law, and to be informed of the nature and cause *(who dropped the dime?)* of the accusation; to be confronted with the ~~witnesses~~ rats against him; to have compulsory process for obtaining witnesses in his favor *(like in the "Godfather" when they brought the wiseguy's brother in)* and to have the assistance of counsel for his defense.

Amendment VII

In suits at common law, where the value in controversy shall exceed twenty dollars *(What are you, nuts? This is gonna be a billion starting today. I can do that, right?)*, the right of trial by jury shall be preserved, and no fact tried by a jury, shall be otherwise reexamined in any court of the United States, than according to the rules of the common law.

Amendment VIII

Excessive bail shall not be required, nor excessive fines imposed, nor cruel and unusual punishments inflicted. *(Let's lose this one altogether — really.)*

> 'No soldier shall, in time of peace, be quartered in any house, or any of my hotels or resorts, without the consent of the owner.'

Amendment IX

The enumeration *(is this some kind of math?...WTF?)* in the Constitution, of certain rights, shall not be construed to deny or disparage others retained by the people. *(You know what? This one's gone, too!)*

Amendment X

The powers not delegated to the United States by the Constitution, nor prohibited by it to the states, are reserved to ~~the states respectively, or to~~ *(you guessed it)* Me, The President ~~the people~~. ∎

TrumpTIME   9

My Briefs

▶ POWER POLITICS

From the cradle to the Oval: my journey.

by President-Elect Donald K. Trump

WHEN I LOOK BACK AT MY AUTOBIOGRAPHY and all the challenges I overcame to get to where I am sitting right now in this great big Corinthian leather chair, I am very, very impressed. Impressed by my smarts, my brains, my unselfishness, my humility and my willingness to do literally anything it takes to get the deal done. This is the mark of greatness, I'm told by authorities who know about these things. So, as a thank you note to the billions who elected me, I offer this inspirational allegory so you can see exactly how much I deserve to be where I am today.

This Boy's Life

I BEGAN TO BE ME AT THE AGE OF ONE. My nanny, who used to sneak a sip from her flask when she thought no one was looking, got a bit hammered and tried to slip me some supermarket baby food. I'm telling you right now, if you're used to hand-strained Bartlett pears for breakfast and someone gives you Gerber's liquid turkey, you're gonna make a stink—and I did. Out of both ends. At that exact moment two things happened: She never pulled that one again and I won my first negotiation.

One of the biggest milestones in my life was when I discovered that there were other people in the world. This happened in third grade at my grammar school in Queens. I caught Bobby Ludnisky stealing the gold-colored crayon out of my Crayola set. Normally, I would have pitched a hissy fit, but I remembered my father saying, "You're turning into a tiny little pussy right before my eyes." So I manned up big time later that day and called

The Hooper triplets looked very, very different than the last time I saw them.

Ludnisky out to the playground. Unfortunately, he sucker-punched me in my hair. This was just too much, so I smartly retreated to the coal bin in our basement. But I never forgot that little Pollack. I've got the IRS looking into Bobby's case.

Boyhood to Manhood

IN 9TH OR 10TH OR 11TH GRADE, I THINK, I LEARNED ABOUT WOMEN and how to appreciate them properly. One sunny day, I was walking by the public swimming pool in Hollis, Queens, on my daily tour of the neighborhood, looking for bank-owned foreclosures to tell my father about, when I happened to notice the Hooper triplets in the pool. They looked very, very different than the last time I saw them. Right away, I got this feeling like you get when you accidentally fall out of bed, followed by a nervous commotion in my trousers. So I ran home, grabbed one of father's *National Geographic* magazines and went to my room to learn about interesting women from all over the world.

The Assent to Power

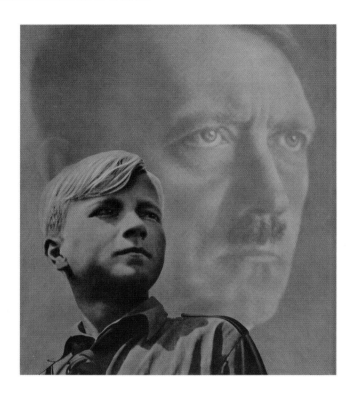

THERE CAME THE DAY, as a young man, when I felt myself growing stronger, gaining power and getting the first inkling that I could be master of my world. I read everything I could understand about the great men of history, the men who changed everything. They all had a few key things in common: They were pure of heart, they were clear of vision, and they knew that they needed to be surrounded by the right people, even if sometimes they would have to eliminate a few lesser individuals along the way.

I felt myself growing stronger, gaining power and getting the first inkling that I could be master of my world.

"It's Just Business, Nothing Personal"

WHARTON BUSINESS SCHOOL taught me one thing and one thing only: how to add up a bunch of numbers and how to kill to make a profit. This place wasn't any fun at all. As I'm sure you can imagine, there wasn't a single woman above a "4," and that's being kind—a concept I heard about recently. My father paid my tuition but I had to somehow pay for gas and assignments to copy, so I used dad's credit line, bought a disaster of a building and turned it into a super-luxury dorm. It would be my first real estate development. I called it the Trump Deluxe Dormitory and Business Spa. It sold out in 41 minutes—a record for any student-owned university building that still stands today.

WHEN I BECAME A LITTLE TOO POTENT for my mother and father to handle, and because it had become clear that two commanding officers couldn't coexist under one roof, my parents very, very graciously sent me to military school. Here was a paradise made just for me. I set a speed record for getting promoted by making Lieutenant General in my first semester. I've checked with the Smithsonian Institution and they say that no serviceman has ever risen through the ranks of any army as fast as I did. On graduation day, the school offered me 25 buildable, prime acres and the rank of Chief of Staff if I would stay on. I respectfully declined. I had completed my military obligation to America and now I had worlds to conquer.

GRAND CENTRAL TERMINAL

THE DEAL I MADE MY BONES ON was built on the back of one of New York City's most embarrassing wrecks, Grand Central Station. By the time I took a look at this mess, the once-great hub of transportation had become a bathroom stop for hookers. But I didn't see it as the pus-oozing sore it was, but as the brand-new, gleaming Trump International Hotel that nobody in New York could afford a room in. Not only did I build a very, very clean shrine and make this dream come true, but I got the city to pay all the taxes until the year 3000 or my death, whichever comes first. This is the formula I now use on all my deals. First, I get somebody to pay every penny of the building costs, then I put my name on it and charge them a shitload of rent. Come on, people, I know you love it!

▼

Three Wives' Tails

AS MY LEGEND AND MY FORTUNE GREW, I had to start showing up with a wife so people wouldn't think I was, you know… I had met this Ivana Z-something with 50 letters, from Europe's east coast, at a fundraiser in support of New York City landlords. When I tell you she was gorgeous, I'm not lying. This was one very, very hot Checkoslobokayan peerogee. Problem was, I couldn't understand a fucking word she said except for "The Donald," and that would end up being my cross to bear for eternity or an extremely long time. But she looked good for a while until I met…

This was one very, very hot Checkoslobokayan peerogee. Problem was, I couldn't understand a fucking word she said except for "The Donald."

...MARLA ANN MAPLES, a slippery little fish I discovered while looking through the real estate section of *Wet Hot Submissive Waitress Magazine.* I had my people send a cab for her at my expense and bring her to my special room at Trump Tower so I could see if there was anything I could do to help her in her career. She was so lovely, childlike and innocent, I almost felt like I could be her father—for about a second and a half. Three days later, I opened Page Six in the *New York Post* and saw the now famous headline with the quote from Marla, "The Best Sex I Ever Had!"—at least she got that right. Eventually, the old adage-type saying from a very, very wise man, or maybe a pimp, came true: "No matter how beautiful they are, there's always somebody that's tired of screwing them." That brings us to my third lady, and now America's First Lady and the first female Vice-President...

▼

▲

...MELANIA KNAUSS. I don't know what it is, but every other wife, I marry a chick with an unpronounceable disaster of a name. I met Melania at New York Fashion Week. *Women's Wear Daily* had begged to interview me so they could get a man with an actual schlong to give an opinion on the future of women's fashion. Mostly, I was trying to answer a shitload of gay questions while, at the same time, keeping thousands of fruitcakes from brushing up against me. Suddenly the sea of ponces parted and there stood Melania, a Slovenian smorgasbord if ever there was one. She actually spoke nine languages. Unfortunately, English was not one of them. So, in yet another very, very smart move, I let little Donald do the talking and he got the job done. Now that we are together, I can say with a very, very large amount of gratitude, and growing ultimate respect, that Melania is the tallest woman I ever married.

So there it is, simplified, smoothed out and right up to date, so you people can see it for the thing of beauty that it is. The encyclopedeya guys are already writing, the playwrights are doing their plays and the rappers are rapping. History is the future right in front of me, and I am not looking back!

—President-Elect Donald K. Trump
America, 2016

IN THIS TEMPLE·
AS IN THE HEARTS OF THE PEOPLE
FOR WHOM HE SAVED THE UNION
THE MEMORY OF ABRAHAM LINCOLN
IS ENSHRINED FOREVER

Mr. Trump goes to Washington.

by TIME Architectural Critic Saul Goldweiner

When Irish-born architect James Hoban began designing the White House in 1791, little could he have imagined that his oeuvre of a lifetime would one day be turned into a cheap, Las Vegas-style tourist trap. Well before the 2016 election, Donald K. Trump began ordering teams of architects and designers to repurpose the existing structure and grounds in order to better reflect his tastes, such as they are, as well as turn a profit. Renamed The Trump House, when completed this once-historic and dignified structure will no doubt still attract millions of visitors, but not necessarily the type you'd want in your house.

Below and on the following pages are some of the many spaces designated by President-Elect Trump as "total disaster areas in need of rebranding." They are accompanied, for what it's worth, by his personal instructions to the horde of minions at his beck and call.

Trump House Exterior

A no-brainer. Paint it with 570 gallons of "Trump Highest-Gloss Ultra-Aryan Blond,"
a lead-based product that'll last until some loser terrorist blows the place up.

Rose Garden

Half-a-brainer. Do you know how much a dozen long-stems go for these days? Just ask a wetback selling them on the side of the road! We can keep the name but let's repurpose this as a cutting garden, with a stand out on Pennsylvania Avenue. Hire a couple of Mexicans to run it—they're good at picking and hawking.

South Lawn

A waste of acreage. Replant the "fairway" with Bermudgrass and the "green" with Bentgrass, following directions found inside the Trump Instamatic Backyard One-Hole Home Golf Course Kit. Golfers will flee Scotland and Augusta and pay a small fortune to play this overnight classic course!

East Room
(formerly the "Public Audience Chamber")

Are you serious? Who would want to attend a function in a room that just faces east? I mean, that's Mecca, right? As the Trump Ball & Blackjacks Room, I've hired the top Vegas casino designers and still-living Shriners to use the top materials to build the best events venue on the planet. I'm gonna blow some foreign dignitaries' minds with the casino that'll go in here—and lap dance all their money while I'm at!

West Wing

Yeah, I watched the show, and it always disturbed me how drab and boring the place looked. I want this space totally gutted and Trumped-out. You've seen Trump Towers, right? Make it look like that.

Situation Room

What situation could be so bad that it'd require its own room and team? Throw these old farts out, gut the place and turn it into a tanning salon.

Treaty Room

I don't sign treaties. Resurface the space in studded leather and rename it the Surrender Room.

Bathrooms

Thirty-five of them? Really? I've never had to go that bad! Whatever, replace all the ancient urinals, toilets, bidets, sinks, tubs and faucets with gold-plated stuff (don't, for god's sake, use the real thing—I'm only gonna be here for eight years!).

Oval Office

Why "oval"? I don't like the name. Makes me think of ovaries, or Ovaltine, or offal (not sure what this is, but I don't like the sound of it). Make this square, like normal offices, replace the portraits of previous occupants with mine, and install a couple of huge-ass flat screens, willya?

Queen's Sitting Room & Bedroom

Freddy Mercury's dead, so why still have a place for him to lay his head when visiting D.C.? Believe it or not, though, there're a lot of flaming fruitcakes in government, especially in Congress. So don't touch anything here in case one of them needs to spend the night! Actually, don't touch a thing in here, period.

James S. Brady Press Briefing Room

Who's James Brady? Wait, wasn't he the dad on that TV show with that little minx of a daughter? If I don't know him, though, he doesn't count. Line the walls with gun racks and call it the "Ted Nugent Shooting Range." We'll sell firearms outta here, too—I mean, it's Washington!

President's Bedroom

Okay, totally blow this space out. Throw away the mattresses—better yet, burn them; power-wash the ceiling, walls, windows and floor; get the Pontiff or pardon some priest in prison to perform an exorcism, then replace the plaster with military-grade mirrored mylar and bullet-proof the shit out of it!

Red Room

Didn't know about this space. I figure it was designed for commies or women running from the Red Scare, but it's the wrong red; it's disgusting. Match it to my ties.

China Room

What the hell's this? What's our trade rival doing with its own room in my house? Oh. Okay, well, I have my own china; it's the very best china, made in China by real Chinese women and child laborers. Sell everything at a tag sale and have a maid or two sleep in here.

Museum/Gift Shop/ Trump & Co. Trumpeteria

A potential cash cow if I ever saw one! Just clear the shelves and restock with my bobbleheads, books, ties, shirts, cufflinks, watches, suits, socks, garters, shoes, slippers, bathrobes, brush and comb sets…what, do I have to spell everything out? Just do it!

Lincoln Bedroom

Another dead guy. I'll tell you something, this room gives me the creeps. All the same, Civil War buffs and Civil Rights wingnuts will pay good money to spend the night here pretending to be assassinated. Leave everything the way it is, including the lumpy, crab-infested (what, you didn't know the kinda woman Mrs. Lincoln was?) horsehair mattress, only rename the space the Lincoln Memorial Presidential Historic Assassination Reenactment Suite. Believe me, we can get a thou a night without spending a dime!

Outgoing Editors' Note: The quotations below would have been forbidden if the Commander/Editor-in-Chief had an attention span longer than a fruit fly's and actually read everything that passes his desk. He doesn't.

"If that flaming A-hole mouths another bad word about my baby Jeb, he'll learn that a bird flipped in the air is better than a Bush in the face. I'm not sure what that means, but I mean it."

BARBARA BUSH, 91, the Kennebunkport, Maine, materfamilias of what would have been a presidential dynasty had her other son not wimped out in the Republican debates.

POPE FRANCIS on Trump's threat to build a wall between Mexico and the United States to deny immigrants ingress.

"MAY GOD TEAR DOWN THE WALL THAT HE HAS ERECTED AROUND HIS HEART. AND IF THAT PRAYER FAILS, THEN *VAFANABOLA, STRONZO!*"

"I'D RATHER DIE THAN SEE HIM BECOME PRESIDENT AND NAME JUDGE JUDY TO THE SUPREME COURT!"

ANTONIN SCALIA, the late arch-conservative Supreme Court Justice on why he was opposed to Donald K. Trump running for the nation's highest office.

"I have long been intrigued by Americans' obsession with themselves but never as intensely as during this year's election. It has been a veritable goldmine for professionals in my field!"

DR. CARL GESELLSCHAFT, the famed Basel, Switzerland, psychiatrist and world-renowned authority on narcissism.

$18.5 million
Trump expenses from start of campaign to election.

$864.64
Cost of the above items manufactured by women and children in third- and fourth-world countries.

$25.5 million
Gross profit from the sale of Trump-branded buttons, banners, beanies, bras, panties, caps, puppets, bobbleheads, etc.

1,000
Number of coats removed during Trump rallies before protesters were thrown out into sub-freezing temperatures between January and March. The garments were later labelled "Exclusive Trump Election Line" and sold on TrumpBay.

"From the dark canyons of a great metropolis, a young child will issue from the loins of rent-hungry people, He who by his tongue, coiffeur and cloven hooves will cast a spell over the masses, rendering them stupider than beasts of burden, more shamed than buggered sheep, more vulnerable than turkeys at Thanksgiving, more…that's as far as I dare foresee."

NOSTRADAMUS, the 16th-century French apothecary, seer and general wingnut writing in *Les Propheties*, published in 1555.

Milestones:

DIED

Bernie Saunders
(early-onset senility)

Mitt Romney
(bored self to death)

Marco Rubio
(drowned in own sweat)

INJURED

Hillary Clinton
(during rough sex)

TRANSGENDERED

Chrissie Cruz
(née Theodore Cruz)

DIGITALS

246*

Estimated number of aliens currently in Congress

245

Number of Republicans in the U.S. House of Representatives.

Brief History

This Month in Time

1657: Heinrich Drumpf of Busendorf, Germany, changes name to Trump in effort to stop local people from calling him "Drummie" and those outside Busendorf ("breasts" in English) from calling him "Tithead."

Heinrich's grandson, Klaus Trump, immigrates to America in 1917, among fellow sheep-buggerers in steerage, aboard the *GodRotterdamn!* Marries Olga and begets Frederick Trump.

Fred Trump meets the future Mrs. Trump and impregnates her with, in his words, "the Bad Seed."

Donald K. Trump, age three months, throws first Trumpertantrum.

Donnie Trump, 8, is suspended from P.S. 01 for holding auditions for Ms. Nude Elementary School pageant.

Donnie Trump, 10, opens lemondade stand, hires Latino kids from the Bronx to wash paper cups. Not able or willing to pay them, files for bankruptcy for the first time.

Don Trump is sent to military school, where he excels at Monopoly and onanism. Later tells reporters that during the war, he mastered his unit.

Dropping out of college, Trump seeks deferment from the military under D-1K (chronic bedwetting)

Donald K. Trump joins Elizabeth Trump & Sons and on same day unseats father as head of the company.

"The Donald" enters the lexicon and Americans' collective unconscious, against their will.

Donald K. Trump marries Melanija Knavs, he for the third time, she for… no one is sure, since she speaks no English and has no papers.

The Donald acquires a 51-percent share of a property spun off by Time-Warner and renames it "*TrumpTIME.*

Donald K. Trump becomes the 45th President of the United States. The next day, two million Americans apply for citizenship in Canada and Mexico.

Donald K. Trump takes first dump as President-Elect.

PRESIDENTIAL PARDONS

Bernard Madoff
(needed in Department of the Treasury)

Ted the "Unabomber" Kaczynski
(needed in war on ISIS)

Pete Rose
(needed back in baseball and Trump casinos)

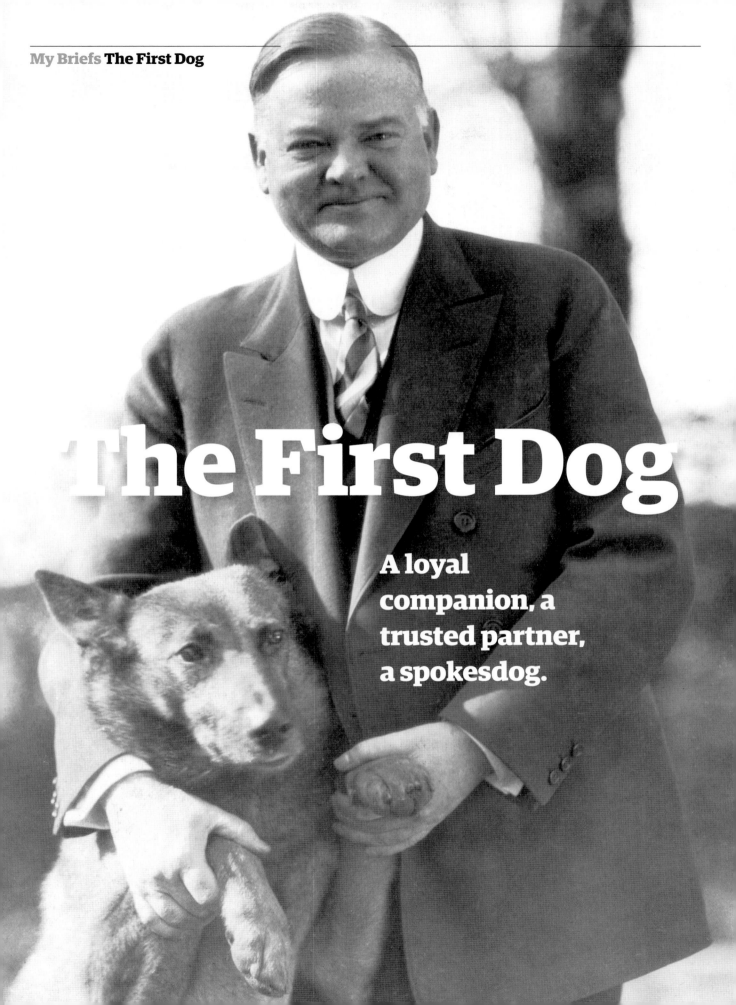

The First Dog

A loyal
companion, a
trusted partner,
a spokesdog.

Even before I took The White House, I knew that the single most important task for an incoming president would be to get a dog that looked good on TV. This had to be done right because historically, in the past, there have been some total disasters in this area. George Washington's Miniature Butthound, Sweetlips, comes to mind. So I radiated my full attention on the audition process by having the Chairman of the Board of Farina Attack Dog Chow, Louise Masterly, suggest a trainer she had an ongoing relationship with.

He came highly recommended.

ELLIE BUTCHERSON KENNELS brought two candidates. The first was a six-year-old Rottweiler named Agent Orange, just back from two years of sniper-ferreting and water-board training in Pakistan.

THIS GUY HAD THE REAL GUNG-HO THING going and breath that stunk like a butcher shop in Calcutta. And very, very disturbingly, he had a 2000 mg a day Oxycontin habit. My people at the Centers for Disease Control tell me that anything over 500 mg a day and it's just a matter of time till you're on an episode of *Cops*. Not only did he not make the cut, but my damn Secret Service detail had to dart him with a hippopotamus tranquilizer to get him out of the building.

His breath smelled like an open air meat market in Calcutta.

A world champion bitch.

NEXT UP, A WORLD CHAMPION FRENCH POODLE BITCH with the name *Mademoiselle Violetta D'Urbanville Comte de Faux-Pas*. Jesus…the French, I'm telling you! Just imagine this bitch prancing around the Oval Office sniffing the Joint Chief's balls while I'm trying to concentrate on bombing somebody! Total loser. Next …

A breeder I could get behind.

FINALLY, A BREEDER THAT MADE SENSE TO ME. Bobbi Jane Winsome of Bobbi's Bad Boys & Bitches Kennel in Austin, Texas, brought the perfect candidate.

Kingmaker I should live until the end of my first term; then I'll swap him out for Kingmaker II.

MEET THE NEW FIRST DOG, eight-year-old AKC Champion, Kingmaker I (I figure he'll die during my first term so this name clears the way for Kingmaker II in my second term.) This stunning Golden Retriever's bloodline apparently goes back more than a hundred years to prehistoric Scotland. I was delighted to discover that my mother's ancestral family actually bred this dog's great-great-great-great-grandfather, Wee Willie. Very, very impressive. Did you notice the color of his hair? There are no coincidences in politics.

Women who are bleeding our country dry.

by President-Elect Donald K. Trump

LOOK, I LIKE WOMEN. I've had plenty of them. Ask any of my golfing buddies like Tiger Woods, Ted Nugent or Bill Cosby (innocent, by the way, I mean, look who his accusers are). They'll tell you I only use the best, the cream of the crop, so to speak, and these are guys who understand women. Women can get a lot done, just ask any executive who's sat in a meeting with my daughter, Ivanka; they'll tell you they can't remember anything else about that day after she walked in the room with those double-Ds. This is the power of women when it's used for the good. And they can have children. We definitely need them for that.

Having said that, in business, politics and roller derby, there are going to be stupid, fat women who drag down the curve. But since this is America, even sloppy losers still deserve a shot. Now, I am a fair man. You can ask anybody if I'm fair. Head NFL referee Pete "Mosey" Moserson thinks I'm fair and who would know better than him? But that disgusting porker, Rosie O'Donnell, shouldn't be allowed to wear a skirt ever again, not that she does now. And the yammering with that mouth and the show biz and those 20 spoiled adoptees from who knows where, with the shaky birth certificates. God knows what goes on in that bedroom. I can't even think about it. This is the kind of unattractive American we just don't need wrecking it for everybody else.

AND MEGYN KELLY. From what I hear from my sources—and these are the very best sources—she was an unsuccessful cheerleader, a real disaster who apparently had something to do with an STD outbreak at her high school that crippled the football, baseball and lacrosse teams, causing permanent damage and knocking all three teams out of the state finals. This is who we want moderating a Presidential debate? I don't think so. She should keep that cat in the cage and go sell bimbo-flavored Girl Scout Cookies, as far as I'm concerned.

WOMEN USUALLY TELL THE TRUTH. I've asked some of the very best women about this and to a man they told me, "Absolutely, women tell the truth." So, I ask you, how could Carly Fiorina have run Hewlett-Packard, the world's greatest computer ink company, right into the ground, a total disaster, in less than a couple of cycles of the moon if she wasn't lying about her performance 100% of the time? Their stock went from millions of dollars a share to about five cents. Of course, that's when I bought it in yet another sweet deal. Now, she's playing with her Barbies and I'm a majority stockholder. Listen, it's women like these that hurt our country. They all want to talk about everything. That's trouble, and trouble in my world means anything that increases the time it takes for me to get a check. If you really look at it—and I have—what are they doing? They're just taking up space doing bad impersonations of men! Like a bunch of drag kings, if you get my point. But in general, I have to say, and everybody will tell you, that I really like women. ∎

My View

▶ **THE ECONOMY**

Creating jobs:
A modest proposal.

**by President-Elect
Donald K. Trump**

AS PROCLAIMED ON THE CAMPAIGN TRAIL, I love the poorly educated. I also happen to love children. Which means I love poorly educated children. And they'll love me back when I let them out of school and give them practical, real-world educations.

As President, that will take place not in concentration camp-like classrooms—where I wasted my entire childhood struggling to concentrate—but out in America's factories, steel mills, construction sites, fishing vessels, logging camps, coal mines, chicken farms and cattle ranches. Childhood experts tell us kids should spend more time outside. I couldn't agree more! Once all the illegal immigrants who've been sucking free milk out of Liberty's tits are gone, there'll also be thousands of jobs for kids in the fields, groves, timberlands and orchards.

Kids don't know about unions—so don't tell them! And under my proposal, they'll never find out. 'Cause in addition to introducing the next generation to reality, I'll save America billions a year in money currently wasted on teachers' salaries. I mean, I never learned a thing in school—even in my history, my favorite subject—and apparently neither did most people who voted for me. So what are we paying teachers for? To stand in front of a room all day talking out of their

asses and writing some stuff on the blackboard or whiteboard or whatever color they are today? Guess what? That free ride's over! Get real jobs, like building world-class luxury condos and apartment buildings or being President!

In brief, my jobs-creation initiative will be a win-win. Kids don't eat much and don't need much money, so we don't have to raise the minimum wage, which is already too high in my opinion. In fact, I'll lower the minimum wage to out-price those slimeball factory owners in China or Bangledish or wherever my shirts and ties are made. I'll also lower the minimum work age to…when do kids start school? Right…to five. Before long, whaddya think's gonna happen? Other countries will be sending their manufacturing jobs to us. Why? Because their kids won't be able to compete against our kids!

Meanwhile, their parents will be free to pursue their own dreams and careers and fortunes, just as I pursued mine once I dropped out of college. Had I left school earlier, I'd be even richer than I am now—and I'm very, very, very rich! What's more, as a private citizen, I created tens of thousands of jobs. I also fired thousands of workers, but that's not the point. My point is that in the process I also created some of the most iconic icons in the world. Not that anyone else can attain what I have, but it should serve as an example of what is possible in life. At least, I mean, in my life. ∎

You totally loved me!

by President-Elect Donald K. Trump

The winners of the Ohio 3H Club Get Behind Trump Bake Sale and Wet Bikini Pageant.

Someday, in the future, history will look back on my presidential campaign and compare it to the great campaigns of all time—like "I'd like to teach the world to sing" or "Where's the beef?"—the great moments that define who we are as Americans. Join me now as I take you on a guided tour of "One nation, individual, with liberty and justice for all!"

Big Guns for the Big Gun!

On the eve of the first Republican debate, I spoke to a huge throng of well-wishers from the deck of the great and powerful battleship, the U.S.S. *Iowa*. Standing below her monster guns, I stood erect, feeling the pride and manliness that the men who built her in Iowa must have felt. From the steelworkers with the helmets and the welding things, to the truck drivers that carried her wide load all the way from the cornfields of Iowa to the Pacific Ocean—and even the women who made the lunches—they all played a role in how we beat the crap out of the Japs. But look at us now; we're drowning in Toyotas and fucking Hello Kitty handbags. I promise you, I'll be taking a new slant on these shenanigans!

Speak your piece and our hosts will show you out.

I remember every second of this event so vividly. I think we were in either New Hampshire or Texas. It was a hot night and pretty humid. My hair felt a little heavy with the moisture so I gave an abbreviated oratory. Honestly, I could have said anything because, as usual, every person there totally loved me—except for a bunch of losers in the back with signs. This kind of crybaby, weenie behavior is the reason America is losing. Losing to China and Mexico, losing to France and Scotland, losing to Russia and fucking Bermuda. Then some whack job in the back asks me, "Mr. Trump, what are you going to do about it?" Realizing this was a trick question, I replied, "Get security!"

The Trump Ghurka Hospitality Squad

Sometimes the crowds and the adulation and the fawning and the kowtowing have to be manhandled, so I usually bring along my own security guys. These gentlemen are my elite Ghurka Hospitality Squad, trained in Nepal in an oxygenless environment. They can sometimes appear stern, so I took some advice from Indian peacenik and expensive shrink Deepak Chopra on how to soften up their image. He suggested Boy Scout kerchiefs in Trump Red to promote breast cancer awareness. People totally loved it.

A Nosh for Peace

Although I seldom sleep or eat in public, I thought a lunch with a rabbi at the world-famous Katz's Deli located in a New York downtown ghetto would help the Jewish voters understand how much I sympathize with their struggle. I think I impressed Rabbi Ari Stern right off the bat by slyly negotiating a table from which I could watch the front door for Arabs or Christians. To loosen things up, I asked the waiter if they had the Gaza Strip Steak. This was funny. But then I ordered brisket for two, figuring the rabbi was cleared for this type of food. Suddenly, though, he seemed to be in a rush to get to a bris or something, so he generously gave me a campaign contribution and called an Uber.

I embody all the best qualities of America.

I embody all the best qualities of America. These are the very deep goodnesses that make this country the hero of the world. I am a walking Rainbow Coalition. I love the black, the brown, the yellow, the red, the tan and the pale. I respect the smart, the stupid and even foreigners to some extent.

Even women get a chance to speak.

I welcomed anybody and everybody to all my rallies, even those with subversive ideas. I gave them all the freedom to speak their piece and then offered helpful, immediate assistance to exit. This was an efficient method to get a good rotation going so the maximum amount of people could feel the warmth of Trump sunshine on their many colors of skin.

The winners of the
Ohio 3H Club
Get Behind Trump
Bake Sale and
Wet Bikini Pageant

They take their animal husbandry and baking very seriously in the Bible Belt. I can't remember a single stop in any of those square-shaped middle states with no cell phone service when somebody didn't come waddling up with a green bean casserole, a red devil Bundt cake or a prize piglet. But I'll tell you one thing: the women entrants of the Get Behind Trump Bake Sale and Wet Bikini Pageant in Smack, Ohio, were strong, muscular, and they knew how to put in an hour's work for a day's pay.

My practice Presidential Cadillac is the Mercedes of Limousines.

While I was out on the trail, I figured I might as well look like I already had the job. And since there's no better symbol of American power than the Presidential Cadillac, I had a practice Caddy made for me by an old sister company of Mercedes-Benz. This four-ton fortress was handcrafted in Germany by Krupp & Putsch, the great arms manufacturer that made those cool—and very, very much ahead of their time—V-2 rockets that made such an impact on London in WWII.

At this stop in South Beach, Florida, I was nearly brought to tears when I saw that even in this tough economic climate, my supporters would literally give me the shirts off their backs. With the patriotic strains of Gloria Gaynor's great American anthem, "I Will Survive," playing in the background, these very, very fit young men joyously lubricated the crowd into a frenzy as the cries of freedom and "Work it bitch!" filled the air. I don't want to blow my own horn, but I've gotta say, nobody does it better.

The cries of "Work it bitch!" filled the air!

The Trump welcome wagon rolls into a town near you!

There came a time on the trail when everybody knew the jig was up, and no matter what, I would soon be their leader. At this point I was, as somebody once said, "more popular than Jesus" and drawing more than Bon Jovi. Now, with millions of Americans coming out to see what the hell just happened, more extreme measures had to be taken for crowd control. As a long admirer of how beautifully the crowds were handled in Chechnya, I asked my pal Vladdy Putin if he could help a brother out with some tactical assistance. So, in exchange for some useless oil rights in Alaska, he sent over a fleet of Trotsky Eliminator recreational vehicles to act as advance ambassadors on my tour. Kids were soon calling them monster trucks. How cool is that!

Election Day Festivities

November 3, 2016, a day that will go down in infamy, or famy, whichever one means famous. It was the day that America woke up to realize that from this moment on, their lives would never be the same. Then the "gatherings" began. I quickly got control and gracefully commandeered the airwaves with the first of my super-positive daily addresses. To set the tone, I coined a phrase from Alexander Haig, Secretary of State and President for six seconds when Reagan got shot, stating that from the tippy top of Maine to the overpriced beaches of Malibu, "I am in control here!" Starting today, the beautiful walls will rise into the sunshine, super-smart deals will be made, people will be well dressed and everybody will do what they're told. It is now 2016 A.T.—After Trump. ■

A Ground-breaking meeting with Vladimir Putin.

 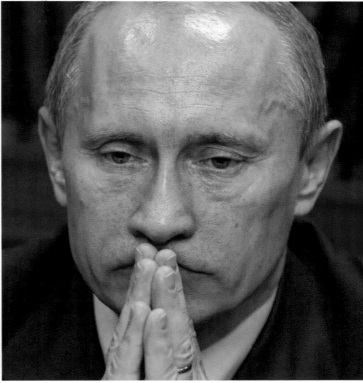

PRESIDENT-ELECT DONALD K. TRUMP turned a surprise visit to New York from Russian President Vladimir Putin, the day after the U.S. elections, into a diplomatic triumph two months before officially occupying the White House! Meeting high above Manhattan in Trump Tower, the new leader of the free world cagily leveraged his home-court advantage to outwit the former KGB chief and broker a deal on the Middle East. What follows is an excerpt from their historic meeting.

T: Welcome to my country, President Putin. I feel that we've known each other for a very long time!

P: We haven't, but yes, already it is seeming like very long time.

> **"Actually, that's a checkerboard, Vlad, which I'm told belonged to President Richard M. Nixon, one of our greatest diplomats—you may have heard of his famous 'Checkers'" speech?"**

T: I agree—it does seem like we've been friends forever. Do I call you Vladimir, or what?

P: My proper name is Vladimir Vladimirovich Putin.

T: That's a lot of Russian in one mouthful, pal! How about I call you Vlad?

P: Vlad is okay. May I call you the Donald?

T: You can call me "Al" if you want! That's an American joke. So, Vlad, thank you for traveling from your frozen, desolate, drunken land to celebrate my landmark victory.

P: So it happens to be visiting residence of mine here.

T: You're kidding! How didn't I know about that? What, is it like a cottage out in Brighton Beach?

P: Ha! You make the Russian joke! No. Last month, in secret transaction, I bought the Chrysler Building. Commanding view from my apartment I can tell you this!

T: Huh! I think I might have owned that property at one point or another. Anyway, what do you think of this place?

P: I like New York very much. Is very desirable city for living—like Moscow only warmer, with good restaurants, good-looking womens and no KGB, only CIA. I make another joke.

T: What I meant was, what about this place—my penthouse apartment—one of the heaviest and most sought-after residences in the world?

P: Is very over-the-head, as expected, my golden friend. But my eyes are drawn to handsome-looking chessboard under one of so many portraits of you. Except there are no pieces. I see a pawn in this room but no king. Where is your king, the Donald?

T: Actually, that's a checkerboard, Vlad, which I'm told belonged to President Richard M. Nixon, one of our greatest diplomats—you may have heard of his famous "Checkers" speech?—and a close personal friend. But I'm sorry to disappoint you.

P: No, no. Opposite is true. Your current President played checkers to my chess last year and the outcome was very favorable. As fate would have it, he turned out to be good friend of the Russian peoples and a supporter of our march again to greatness.

T: I know something about greatness, Vlad! Okay, let's talk, one world leader to another. What are your ambitions in the Middle East?

P: The path to greatness and freedom is never simple. There are tragic and glorious pages in our history.

T: Don't really know what the hell you're talking about. All I know is what my future Secretary of Defense, Ted Nugent, tells me, and that's that you've been expanding your presence in the region.

P: Yes, we have some Spetsnaz on the ground in Syria.

T: And what's this I hear about bombing civilian homes and property in Aleppo, wherever that is?

P: Yes, is true. I do not lie. One of our pilots, trained in United States, accidentally dropped the bombs on Syrian peoples. "My bad," as you say in this country, though in truth I have never heard you say this, the Donald.

T: But what about Iran? Those mo-fos have the means to manufacturer nuclear weapons of mass destruction, taking jobs away from Americans who would kill to make them, and we lift the fucking sanctions against them?! Well, not on my watch! Which begs the question, my Rooskie friend: What's in this for you and your country?

P: Shall we simply say that Russia's destiny is aligned with Iran's, and vice versa. An emerging power free of sanctions will ultimately stalemate certain other countries' regional hegemonic ambitions, especially with respect to Syria. I do not expect you to understand, my ingenuous friend. But in time, believe me, you will.

T: Thank you for that last compliment on my genius, the Vladimir. But let's be specific here, as well as comprehendable. Where do I fit into this scenario? Because I can tell you one thing: Beyond being a huge celebrity and entertainer, I am a very, very successful businessman.

P: How wise of you to sense business opportunity here, the Donald! So now I will tell you. Keeping the sanctions lifted will mean money, and money will mean demand among Iranian peoples for high-end American "goods and services."

T: Go on, Vlad. Like what?

P: Like things such as this flamboyant apartment. Brioni suits like the ones you and I wearing this very moment. Luxury hotels and resorts like you build. Keeping sanctions lifted is good thing for Iran and Russia, good thing ultimately for Syria, and very good thing maybe for you.

T: You have my attention—not an easy thing to do, I can tell you.

P: Property is very cheap and available in region right now. I myself own four square blocks of prime, downtown Aleppo real estate. Condos and casinos might do very, very well there someday.

> **"What about Iran? Those mo-fos have the means to manufacture nuclear weapons, taking jobs away from Americans who would *kill* to make them!"**

T: You mean a world-class casino with a liquor license, scantily clad women and enough gold-plated stuff to outshine the Pharaohs of Egypt.

P: We can call it "Al" if you want, my outlandish and strangely hirsute friend. Just tell me you, as somehow President, you will keep all sanctions lifted.

T: I have no idea what they are but done deal, Vlad!

P: Is good. Now I must travel to Teheran, where other business awaits..

T: Just tell me one thing before you go: How do two great world leaders and close friends say "goodbye" to one another in Russian?

P: *Yebat tvoyu mat!*

T: Thank you, and the same to you ∎

The Trump Cabinet

by *TrumpTIME* Washington Correspondent Wade Winchell

PRESIDENT-ELECT DONALD K. TRUMP today released his list of candidates to head the principal departments of the executive branch of the federal government. As proposed, the Trump Administration's Cabinet posts would draw from among the nation's most seasoned (read "over-the-hill") politicians, famous (or "infamous"—the President doesn't appear to understand the difference) business leaders and figures (both fictional and all too real for comfort) from the entertainment field. One of the greatest challenges the President faced in this serious decision-making process was the naming of his Vice President (some challenge!), as you'll see.

SECRETARY OF STATE

Bill Clinton

FORMER PRESIDENT WILLIAM JEFFERSON CLINTON was an easy choice for this critical Cabinet post. Given his experience in dodging lawsuits, impeachment proceedings and intense judicial and spousal questioning, he is a natural for the sensitive and potentially litigious post. Mr. Clinton's candidacy should not be interpreted as a slight to his wife, the soundly defeated and publicly humiliated Democratic presidential candidate Hillary Clinton.

I know people are going to wonder what I'm thinking here, but with Bill, I get a "twofer." First, I get the sum of all Hillary's experience with state leaders, since he was obviously telling her what to do on all that stuff. And second, I get the benefit of Bill's intimate knowledge of women, what makes them tick and his amazing skill at deniability.
—DT

COMMERCE

Jeff Bezos

JEFFREY PRESTON BEZOS brings a wealth of business cunning and ruthlessness to the post of Secretary of Commerce, earning the President's admiration and respect. As founder and CEO of Amazon.com, Mr. Bezos has done for e-commerce what President-Elect Trump did for politics—"fucked up the competition!" (the President's words, not mine). Whether squashing competitors, suing complainants or bullying publishers, Mr. Bezos's style meshes perfectly with the President's penchant for control while, as a fellow billionaire, sharing the Commander-in-Chief's love of money, power and ultimate world domination.

I'll tell you one thing I really appreciate about this guy: He did what he did with zero hair. Also, how cool is it to sit on your ass, hit a button and the next day you get a case of Axe men's body wipe delivered right to your door (or in my case, the front sentry gate)? —DT

TREASURY

Bernie Madoff

BERNARD L. MADOFF is an acknowledged master of the art of the steal. A former chairman of the NASDAQ and his own securities firm, he almost single-handedly pulled off the largest Ponzi scheme in U.S. history, bilking investors of some $60 billion over the course of more than 20 years. In proposing Mr. Madoff for this post, the President reasons that anyone so good at amassing a fortune and keeping it a secret for so long can keep the nation's wealth safe from America's foreign enemies. (See also "Presidential Pardons," page 24.)

*Sixty F***ing Billion dollars!? I care less about what this guy did than the fact that he could write the biggest personal check in the history of the world. And imagine the air miles! —DT*

DEFENSE

Ted Nugent

THEODORE ANTHONY "TED" NUGENT has long been one of President-Elect Trump's favorite musicians, not to mention a close personal friend. The wildly talented singer-guitarist will bring to the Defense Department a fierce patriotism, a hunter's instincts for ferreting out America's enemies and a personal arsenal of some 1,200 handguns, shotguns, assault rifles, crossbows, flamethrowers and anti-aircraft artillery. In addition to his duties as Secretary of Defense, Mr. Nugent will lead the newly created Department of Offense, drawing upon a position on the NRA board, an abrasive personality and albums used to torture prisoners at Guantanamo.

Here's this guy's average day: He shoots a deer for breakfast, then he spends 15 minutes or however long it takes with his knockout of a wife. Then it's howitzer target practice, kill a wolf for lunch, back with the wife, etc. This is the guy that 100 percent will watch our backs. —DT

ATTORNEY GENERAL
Hal Ripschitz

President-Elect Trump's first choice for the top legal post is legendary litigator Hal Ripschitz, a fierce advocate of individuals' right to make inflammatory, derogatory, retaliatory statements with impunity. In private practice, he defended celebrated loudmouths Don Imus, George Steinbrenner and Charles Barkley. In the Cabinet, he'll largely be responsible for defending the President.

"The guy's last name alone qualifies him as the kind of Attorney General this Administration's gonna need! —DT

INTERIOR

Gianni Caravaggio D'Oro

The famed Italian interior designer is well known to President-Elect Trump, having decorated his $100-million penthouse in Trump Tower, which has been rightly called "the heaviest apartment in Manhattan." As Secretary of the Interior, Mr. D'Oro's mission from the President-Elect is to Trumpify the "fruited plains" between Los Angeles and New York, including the national parks and wilderness areas.

Having been informed by my staff that every President needs a sensitive visionary, I picked this guy up. I am really looking forward to putting him in a scout uniform and sending him to spruce up Yosemite. —DT

HOMELAND SECURITY
Metal Man

Tommy Bark captured the President's attention in the *Metal Man* franchise of top-grossing, C-Movie films. The combination of super powers and super wealth resonates with the President's view of himself, while addressing his need to protect his assets—along with other rich Americans'—from villains, both domestic and foreign.

First, you gotta love that suit. I'll tell you, if I could fly around blowing shit up, O'Donnell's house would be a hole in the ground! —DT

VICE PRESIDENTIAL RUNNERS-UP

Sarah Palin Endorsed Donald K. Trump during his campaign, and sexy in a homicidal librarian kind of way, but the thought of her assuming presidential powers in an emergency gives even the President the willies.

Tina Fey Smarter than the first runner-up by miles but a little too smart and sassy for the President's temperament. In addition, he frequently gets her and Palin confused.

Jeb Bush Fulfills the primary requirement of the office to do nothing, but considered too much of a non-entity for even a cameo role.

Joe Lieberman A political party cross-dresser, appealing to both sides of the aisle, but not someone the President would feel comfortable having stand behind him. Nor near him. That he's still alive is even discomforting.

Mark Cuban A highly successful businessman and sports team owner whose brashness and wealth might make him a formidable ally of the President's. His surname and loser team standings, however, ultimately eliminated him from the running.

Please see next page for the next Vice President of the United States! ▶

THE VICE PRESIDENT

Melania Knauss Trump

A SLOVENIAN-BORN FORMER MODEL and watch and jewelry designer, Melania Trump embodies many of the qualities the Commander-in-Chief admires in a Vice President.

The Slovenian met the future President in 1998 at a Fashion Week party and later, modeling for a number of agencies including Trump Model Management, was featured in a bikini in the 2000 Sports Illustrated Swimsuit Issue, in the process confirming Mr. Trump's valuation of her assets. Although fluent in Slovenia, Serbian, German, French and Trumpish, she is best known for saying nothing.

More than a woman.

Excerpt from *59 Minutes* television interview with America's First Lady Vice-President with special correspondent Bizzy Dailey.

59: Good afternoon, Madame Vice-President, and thank you so much for sitting down to talk to us today.

M: Hello.

59: Americans are curious to know how you plan on managing the stress of two very demanding jobs, First Lady and Vice-President of the United States.

M: Thanks you. It's Givenchy Couture.

> **Ali govorite slovensko? This is Slovenian for "Do you speak Slovenian?"**

59: Yes, I see. There's no question that you are a woman of great style and taste. Do you think these qualities will be helpful in the rough and tumble men's world of international politics?

M: I am here now exactly and will fix every total disasters to make them cute again. This is job number one.

59: If you would, please put on your Vice-President's hat for a minute and tell our viewers some of your thoughts on the topic of women's rights.

M: Okay, give me hat.

59: Mmmm. Let me shift the direction slightly. Americans haven't been exposed to much Slovenian culture. What would you like them to know about the rich history of your country?

M: Story of Naughty Prkmndclk from Lzdhndro. Scary for bedtime, good for sexytime.

59: Speaking of time, I see we're out of it, Madame Vice President. I want to thank you and wish you luck in the coming months and years.

M: Ali govorite slovensko? This is Slovenian for "Do you speak Slovenian?"

59: This is Bizzy Dailey with America's First Lady. Good night, and God help us all.

Living the American dream, Trump-style.

by President-Elect Donald K. Trump

I have wanted things for as long as I can remember. The best things. Today, everything I own, everywhere I live, everything I wear, everything I eat and everything I marry is the absolute finest. And the sum of all these glorious parts is what the best people call...Trump Style!

My Clothes.

THERE HAS NEVER BEEN A PRESIDENT WHO COULD CARRY MY SHORTS when it comes to looking presidential. They say clothes make the man; well in my case, the man makes the clothes—in sizes up to 6X Portly, Big & Tall, available nationwide except Macy's which is a loser. I gotta tell you, when it comes to sartorialness, I am very, very there. As a matter of fact, a recent poll said that Trump brand clothing literally beat the crap out of Jerry Armani and Puff Diddy as one of the most trusted names in American fashion.

THE SUITS I WEAR personally are tailored from 105% super six hundred worsted wool, hand woven by Scottish crones in peat moss huts in the village of Dingwall. This fabric is carried by armed courier to my tailor, Sidney "the needle" Finklestein, in New York, who keeps three manikins in differing sizes to accommodate any changes in my physique due to humidity, banqueting or deals gone south. Sidney's process is totally meticulous, very, very lengthy, and is interrupted only by his daily dialysis sessions. The result is a suit that has the power to silence a room full of enemies or a noisy woman.

MY SHIRTS ARE CRAFTED from 850 thread count South Sea Island cotton, hand dyed on a South Sea island to achieve my custom color of Trump White. This color is, I'm told by my physicists, designed to never "blow out," distort or vibrate under television lights. The shape of the collar has been aero tested in a wind tunnel to ensure zero lift in winds up to 100 miles

an hour (a note about my hair later). By the way, I've been assured by NASA that this is a wind speed record for any shirt—ever!

THE DONALD K. TRUMP SIGNATURE MODEL RED TIE, another iconic item I will be remembered for, is the densest and heaviest tie in the world, weighing in

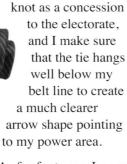

at over one pound. I use the Republican-style tie knot as a concession to the electorate, and I make sure that the tie hangs well below my belt line to create a much clearer arrow shape pointing to my power area.

As for footwear, I wear my personal brand, Trump Dealmaster Brogues, exclusively. These are fashioned from Okinawan Kobe beef hides tanned in Borsalino, Italy, with the finest opera music playing in the background. To protect the secrets of their construction, they are finished by blind shoemakers in Flushing, Queens, and delivered to my office in a Brinks truck, ensuring that absolutely nobody will walk in my shoes.

The Hair.

Let's get this over with once and for all. Number one, it's all mine, and it's very, very unique. To make absolutely sure of its pedigree, I've had the DNA checked, which you can do at Ancestry.com on TV. The numbers don't lie, folks. On my mother's side, this golden hair goes all the way back to the MacLeod clan in ancient Scotland from before, almost, fire. To answer the next obvious question: Yes, the cuffs and collar match. I wear the hair in my signature bouffant style for two reasons. First, it's exceptionally good looking and it gives me a youthful, music loving, "making the scene" type appearance in the vein of the blonde guy in *Zoolander*. Second, and most important, it's much more manageable in high winds. Luckily, now that I'm the President, I can have the venues of my speech appearances cleared by meteorologists.

Gilding My Lilies—My Personal Homes.

From Mar-a-Lago in Florida to the Trump Ice Palace in north Greenland, there isn't a place anywhere on earth where I can't get to one of my thousands of personal beds in 15 minutes. I personally own over 600 homes worth nearly a trillion dollars. This is something that nobody, not even Genghis Cohen, another real estate mogul,

could say. The centerpiece of my collection is, of course, Trump Tower, where I have my office and my three-story private penthouse worth, at last count, two billion dollars. I took my decorating cue here from the Palace at Versailles but way, way more grand. There isn't a single inch, from floor to ceiling, in the entire apartment that isn't made out of something either very, very expensive, extinct or, wait for it, solid gold. I have my maids strip searched on their way out every day.

Then I've got the Fluge compound in Virginia, now known as Trump Vineyard Estates. I am particularly proud of this property for several reasons, the most important being that it was formerly owned by the richest man in America, Juan Fluge. Here's how this very, very smart deal unfolded. I hung around till he went bankrupt —they always do—and died. Next, I waited for the bank to foreclose on his widow. While that was going on, I secretly bought the front and back yards, sprinkled some rusty old trailers and barbecues around and let the grass grow six feet tall. This basically killed the property. Then,

in one of my favorite deals ever, I snagged it from the bank for $15,000. Now it's a national landmark decorated in the style of Egyptian Pharaoh Nefertitty, and is probably one of the most beautiful residences in the world with an appraised value of several billion dollars. ∎

Inherit the wind!

by Deputy Press Secretary P.J. Salinger, IV

ON THE LONG ROAD TO THE WHITE HOUSE, critics of Donald K. Trump enjoyed pointing out that while he was quick to lay bare the problems facing the country, tapping citizens' deepest anxieties and fears, he offered no concrete solutions.

"The future is flatulence."

At the same time, with fracking coming under attack following a number of environmental disasters, the same critics seized on a 2012 tweet in which Mr. Trump allegedly wrote, "Fracking will lead to American energy independence. With the price of natural gas continuing to drop, we can be at a tremendous advantage."

The President has no memory of that tweet. "I've never used the word 'fracking,'" he says, "except maybe in swearing—'I have no fracking idea' or 'You're a fracking idiot!'—so I probably didn't write it, or somebody at Twitter changed it, which is a disgusting thing to do."

What President-Elect Trump most likely meant, if he meant anything at all, was not advocacy of fracking but advocacy of *farting*—the natural gas implied in the phrase "natural gas"—that would free America forever from OPEC's dominance and lead to energy independence for the nation.

What fools such critics be! Had they only looked behind the theatrical curtains of the campaign to see the man I've come to know, admire (and yes, love; there, I've said it!), they would have understood that he was keeping his diplomacy cards close to his vest until he had won the election and could present an energy policy that even his dumbest supporters would be able to understand.

Flatulence is a naturally occurring, renewable resource from cows, some Americans and all Mexicans. Under the soon-to-be-proposed Trump Illegal Aliens Capture & Natural Gas Recapture Act, methane produced in abundance by bovines after grazing and by Mexicans

HUMAN METHANE
EMISSIONS OUTPUT
according to statistics from
the Trump-LaPew Research
Lavatory in conjunction with
The Pinto Bean Association
of North America.

Trump-LaPew found that six
U.S. cities with the highest
emissions of hydrogen sulfide
gas particles parts—or Fart
Parts, in layman's parlance—
per pure air (FPppa)
coincidentally contained
the highest concentrations
of Hispanics.

Brownsville, TX
87.8 FPppa

Salinas, CA
82.3 FPppa

Miami, FL
79.9 FPppa

Los Angeles, CA
78.2 FPppa

Elizabeth, NJ
77.2 FPppa

Bridgeport, CT
63.2 FPppa

"The genius of the Act, once passed, is that it would also overcome two other largely silent but deadly problems: immigration and jobs creation."

after bean-infused meals would be collected at methane centers in strategically located cities *(see chart, left)*. There, engineers would hook donators up to natural gas pipelines *(see photograph, below)* that, in turn, would feed power stations across the country.

At the same time, the wind generated by these natural methane producers would power windmills located in American cities already redolent of immigrants before sending the airborne effluent in the direction of OPEC countries.

The genius of the Act, once passed, is that it would also overcome two other largely silent but deadly problems facing America: immigration and jobs creation. When caught, illegal immigrants from south of the border would be given daily reprieves from deportation. In addition, they would be paid for their methane output from taxes imposed on Mexican restaurants, thereby freeing landscaping and dishwashing jobs for legal American citizens.

But the main thrust of the Trump energy act is power. "Flatulence is the future!" President-Elect Trump declared during a news conference this morning at The Beanery, a fast-fart restaurant in Elizabeth, New Jersey. "Tapping this natural occurrence in Mexicans has the potential to fire up American factories, run farm machinery and automobiles, and send spacecraft to the distant rim of the fracking solar system!" ■

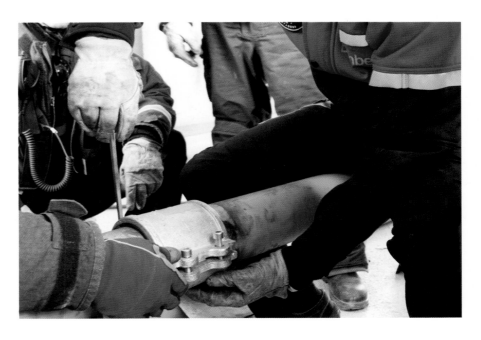

Countries with two or more strikes against them.

At the first morning briefing with the President following the election, we discussed the day's schedule and the POTUS's policy initiatives that I will attempt to interpret and somehow translate into cogent press releases. On this occasion, however, in an effort to be, in his words, "more intimate with my people," President-Elect Trump made me release his thoughts of the day verbatim.
—*White House Press Secretary P.J. Salinger, IV*

Scotland

Here's the deal here. There hasn't been a damn thing happening on this disaster of an island for as long as anybody can remember—all the way back to that Mel Gibson movie with the blue faces. But since my mother was Scottish and I care deeply for these poor people, I thought, "Let's lose the wool skirts and the fucking bagpipes, put big boy pants on them and bring them into the 21st century." Now the obvious way to do that was to build the finest golf course in history with a very, very nice shop where they could sell their whiskey. So I spoke to some authorities on whiskey and golf, and every one of them agreed that my plan would literally save the nation and create 41,000 jobs. Next, I put a killer deal together to buy a mile of mud along the coast to build the Trump International Hebrides (See? I know my geography and stuff!) Upmarket Golf Course & Spirit Shoppe. And what do they do? They shun me, a native son. They put up giant windmills within the view of my clubhouse and wrecked the whole thing. Two strikes and a foul tip!

Arabia

Strike one, who's gonna trust a place where the women walk around wrapped up like burn victims? And I don't like sand. It scuffs up my Trump Dealmaster llama-leather shoes. The whole place is irritating. I also don't enjoy watching camels spitting on tourists; it's disgusting. Look, this place has been around since the Bible—you'd think they'd learn something in a couple of hundred years. And just try sitting in a meeting with a bunch of guys dressed up like Klu Klucks Klan members in white sheets with black doughnuts on their heads. They don't say a damn thing and they all look alike, so how do you know who to impress? But when it comes time to buy their four-wheel-drive Cadillacs and their mile-long yachts with missile launchers, who do they come crawling to? The U.S. of fucking A. The only reason these guys are worth sparing is because they snap up 75-million-dollar penthouses as fast as I can build them.

London, Britain

How do you expect anybody to take you seriously when the whole country looks like it has meth-mouth? Also, those hair hats they wear in court (and they talk about my hair?) make all their politicians and lawyers look like they're in a remake of *Mutiny on the Bounty.* But all that aside, I don't like mutton. And I also don't like the fact that there are more Muslims in London than soldiers in the British Army—an army, by the way, that still has wooden wheels on their tanks and soldiers that still do that dopey little dance when you say "halt!" That cockeyed threat of banning me from showing up over there was squashed when I told them I'd send my dentist—the best tooth man in the world, according to an in-house poll—to straighten out those disasters they speak through. Still…the city and whole country are on probation for the foreseeable future.

France

France has one thing going for it that I can see: The women wear real stockings with seams, like in *Casablanca*. However, I did notice a lot of very, very long, very black leg hair visible through those stockings, and when you combine that with the ripe armpits in the summer, it's easy to see why they invented perfume—and cheese. I made a killing shorting deodorant last year. The other thing bringing them down is that the men are extremely tiny. A French double extra-large men's shirt would be tight on a three-year-old. The wine's OK, but I make way better wine at Chateau Neuf de Trump in Atlantic City. All we really have to do here is stop the flow of Jerry Lewis DVDs—that'll be punishment enough.

Russia

Here's why we don't have to worry about bombing the Rooskies. If the Russians ever get pissed—or drunk enough—to hit the launch button, I'll tell you exactly what will happen: A six-foot-long cardboard "missile" powered by a Roman candle will travel 150 feet and land in a glass of vodka. Then the whole country will go on strike, get hammered and sickled, and pass out. War's over, no bomb. It's this kind of efficient, clear-headed thinking by a cost-conscious leader that separates me from all previous Presidents in American history.

Mexico

Here's the whole Mexican, pain-in-the-asshola mess wrapped up in a burrito that's easy for anyone to swallow. Option one: La Bomba, the easiest one; a call from me and the whole place is as flat as a quesadilla. Problem solved. Option two: More difficult, but very, very smart. First, I'm gonna stop up that flushing toilet called the border with the most beautiful wall since China or that crying one in Israel. This wall will be paid for, not by the government of Mexico, but by the drug cartels. Can you see the beauty of this deal? We give them a legit way to launder their cash, and I won't look too closely for tunnels in the construction plans. Comprende? So, what do we end up with? The exact same amount of drugs coming in—and that's OK since we need them for the guys on Wall Street anyway—but no rapists! A total win-win and I don't have to waste an expensive bomb that could be used on a way more deserving target like Kim Bang Bong in North Korea. ∎

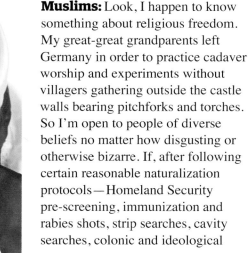

HELP WANTED
NO IRISH NEED APPLY

Immigration: This land is my land.

by President-Elect Donald K. Trump

FIRST, I WANT TO THANK ALL OF THE MEXICANS who voted for me in this long and at times testy presidential campaign.

I know I said some things along the way that may have offended your country of origin. But I also want you to know that you still have your jobs landscaping, share-cropping, dishwashing, housekeeping, janitoring, etc. on my properties and in my apartments, houses, casinos, spas, nightclubs, golf clubs, strip clubs, etc. around the country.

Staying true to my campaign statements, however, I want to assure my Anglo constituents that none of the Mexicans in my employ are rapists or murderers or illegals. At least not that I'm aware of. I mean, I don't know, how would I know? I never asked and, had they told me, I wouldn't have understood because I don't speak the Español and never will, this is America after all, not the United States of Empañadas!

But immigration remains a very, very serious issue for this great nation of ours. Believe it or not, my own family immigrated to this country, though centuries ago and when immigrants were white—call us "white-backs," if you wanna call us names—and, rather than "fleeing" something or another, they came here "seeking" a better life for… me, ultimately and mainly.

To make America great again—in other words, "more like the country of my people and me"—I forthwith propose a number of measures that will both ensure the xenophobic integrity of our nation and continue to serve as the land of opportunity for opportunists. As the famous Emma of Lazarus poem engraved at the base of the Statue of Liberty proclaims, "Give me your cunning, your brash, your greedy and narcissistic yearning to take advantage of your huddled masses."

Hispanics: Look, let's decide about these people on a case-by-case basis. Are you able and willing to work long hours in the broiling sun or in baking kitchens performing mindless physical labor no legitimate Americans are willing to do? Fine. You're in.

Muslims: Look, I happen to know something about religious freedom. My great-great grandparents left Germany in order to practice cadaver worship and experiments without villagers gathering outside the castle walls bearing pitchforks and torches. So I'm open to people of diverse beliefs no matter how disgusting or otherwise bizarre. If, after following certain reasonable naturalization protocols—Homeland Security pre-screening, immunization and rabies shots, strip searches, cavity searches, colonic and ideological purging, ESL classes and the new SAT exam—Muslims are still living, they are welcome to apply for American citizenship.

Slovenians: Have you seen my wife? Not her—the third and current one, Melania? Then you know what we're looking for in immigrants from this country, wherever that is. You're female and you look like her? Fine, you're in. You're male, or female with male-like characteristics—mustaches and chin hair, flat and/or hairy chests, backs like oxen, underarm hair long enough to braid, B.O., prominent moles or other outgrowths—better stay where you're appreciated for your abilities to plow fields, haul wood and water, and bear lots of little Slovenians. 'Cause you ain't coming here!

Catholics: Until "Papa" repents and apologies to me for questioning my faith—publicly and to my satisfaction—no number of indulgences or prayers to St. Jude are gonna help your cause. Believe in me!

British: I don't think so—not with those teeth, not to mention your government's suggestion that I not be allowed in your cross-dressing, fish 'n' chips-eating, sun-has-set-on-the-empire domain!

Scots: Abso-f'ing-lutely not! Go scoff down some haggis while listening to dirges and stare at windmills all day long!

Irish: If there's a job opening for anything other than bartender, cop or Boston political boss, the old signs in the windows stand: "No Irish need apply."

Foreign Women: Again, on a case-by-case basis. Seeing how I'm really the only one qualified to judge these cases, as each appears before me in the Oval Office—close the door behind you, please!—I'll be the judge and jury. Next! ■

Donald K. Trump @DonaldTrump — Follow

I'm in! 146 million Americans took the pledge, and no, it's NOT a nazi salute

9:36 PM - 10 Mar 2016   #Koolaid #Munich

105,945   152,316

Myley Cyrus @MyleyCyrus — Follow

Kool it haters, daddy will take care of us!

9:36 PM - 10 Mar 2016   #Badlittlegirl
#NaughtyNaughtyBaby

105,945   152,316

Geraldo Rivera @Stillrelevant — Follow

I'm on Dancing With the Stars. You couldn't do the Macerana if your hair depended on it.

9:36 PM - 10 Mar 2016   #I'm a real journalist
#taller than you think.

105,945   152,316

Arianna Huffington @Huffingtonpost — Follow

I'm opening my window on the 14th floor. Goodbye and good luck.

9:36 PM - 10 Mar 2016   #End of days #5,4,3,2,....

105,945   152,316

Donald K. Trump @DonaldTrump — Follow

Rivera? That's a Mexican name right?

9:36 PM - 10 Mar 2016   #Green card #Drug cartel

105,945   152,316

Donald K. Trump @DonaldTrump — Follow

Typical chick overreaction. But anyway so long loser.

9:36 PM - 10 Mar 2016   #Fugly #Badhair

105,945   152,316

Vladimir Putin @Ukraine top this — Follow

I love you, The Donald. We will make much dollars together.

9:36 PM - 10 Mar 2016   #Wet kiss to Melania
#vodka #crackpipe

105,945   152,316

Rosie O'Donnell @50kids and counting. — Follow

Yes, that was me on the White House lawn you fuck. I'm coming for you Trump.

9:36 PM - 10 Mar 2016   #Girlpower #Tinyhands

105,945   152,316

Donald K. Trump @DonaldTrump — Follow

None of you total disaster losers matter. I am here, now is then, the future is in very, very big hands!

9:36 PM - 10 Mar 2016   #How do you like me now Ivanka?

105,945   152,316

TrumpTIME Magazine Book Reviewer **Alicia Mayhem** sat down with President-Elect Donald K. Trump shortly after the election to talk about his latest work, *Profiles in Cleavage.*

The title of your new book comes uncomfortably close to John F. Kennedy's *Profiles in Courage.* Were you inspired by his tome?

Actually, I've never visited JFK's tomb and never read his book, so I can't answer that. But I wrote *my* book—and, by the way, I'm a very, very good writer—to respond to critics who claim I don't like women. In fact, I love women, especially women with great cleavage. So with this book I hope to put that misconception to bed. The main thing is that every great President has written a book. Look, you've got George Washington's *The Cherry Orchard…*

That was Chekhov.

You've got George W. Bush's autobiography of his brother, *The Idiot…*

That was Dostoyevsky.

You've got George Foreman's…I forget what he wrote but I have one of his grills, which he had custom-made for me. It's a terrific grill, it's a terrific book and he's a terrific guy.

Who do you see playing you if this were made into a porn film?

Well, I have to say—and I think you'll agree—that there's no one on the face of the Earth better suited to play me than me. As for the women I pay my respects to in the book, I'd have to go with a classic, like Jayne Mansfield, and of course my daughter. Believe me, between the two of them there's enough cleavage to fill an IMAX screen!

What books are on your nightstand?

The better question is, "What *is* your nightstand?" I have many, actually, given the number of homes I own, and all are made out of volumes from my collected

works. They have been stacked, compressed, glued and hand-shellacked to a velvety sheen in order to create the most unique, as well as one-of-a-kind, nightstands on the market. There are no better nightstands for standing next to a bed at night.

Back to your writing. Forgive me, Mr. President, but I've read your books and, frankly, a drunk monkey could hunt-and-peck better sentences.

What about *War and Peace*? You're telling me you didn't like that one? Come on—it's like one of the most famous books in the anals of American literature.

But that's a Russian novel and you didn't write it! Leo Tolstoy did.

Are you sure? Because I'm pretty sure I did. "War" and "Peace"—I remember writing both words down during my campaign. Now Leo Gorskey, maybe he could've written it, but some guy named Leo Tolstoy? Seriously? What kinda name is that? Sounds like a Russian vodka and I never touch the stuff.

Is it possible that your literary sensibilities have been "influenced" by your pal Vladimir Putin?

I believe we've deeply influenced one another. Frankly, he's a huge fan of my literary output. As he told me just yesterday, "It seems, the Donald, that the fox has gotten into the publishing house!" ∎

Acknowledgements

The authors would like to thank the following people
for their friendship, encouragement and support:
Norman Lear, Robert Downey, Jr., Alan Neigher and Bill Raveis.

Special thanks are due our great editor, Gretchen Young, and
the supporting cast at Grand Central Books and Hachette:
Beth deGuzman, Jamie Raab, Katherine Stopa, Chris DuBois
and their fearless leader, Michael Pietsch.

We are indebted—and have been for many years—to our designer,
the wonderful Laura Campbell of campbell + company graphic design.

Finally, we extend our warmest appreciation to Donald Trump:
Parodists' dream, advocate of unfiltered free speech and,
keeping in mind the adage that imitation is the sincerest form of flattery,
the good sport we know he will be.

Photo Credits:

Page 3, feature story, A. Katz/Shutterstock.com; Get Behind Trump girl, Dan Holm/ Shutterstock.com. Pg 5, Trump profile, Crush Rush/Shutterstock.com. Pg 12, Hitler Youth poster, Everett Historical/Shutterstock.com. Pg 13, cadets marching, Free Wind 2014/Shutterstock.com. Pg 14, Ivana Trump, Featureflash/Shutterstock.com. Pg 15, Marla Maples, Vicki L.Miller/Shutterstock.com; Melania Trump, Featureflash/Shutterstock.com. Pg 18, woman with roses, Paul Prescott/Shutterstock.com; Oval office, Joseph Sohm/Shutterstock.com. Pg. 20, Queen's br, Andrey Shcherbukhin/ Shutterstock.com; gift shop, ChameleonsEye/Shutterstock.com. Pg 22, Lincoln br, Nina Leen/The LIFE Picture Collection/Getty Images; Pg 23, Pope, Neneo/Shutterstock.com. Pg 24, Transgender model, zadirako/Shutterstock.com; Trump caricature, LifetimeStock/ Shutterstock.com. Pg 25, Hoover & dog, Library of Congress/Getty Images. Pg 29, Rosie O'Donnell, s_bukley/Shutterstock.com; Megyn Kelly, Craig Barritt/Getty Images for Cosmopolitan Magazine and WME Live; Carly Fiorina, Christopher Halloran/Shutterstock.com. Pg 30, child workers, Borthwick Institute/Heritage Images/Getty Images. Pg 31, empty schoolroom, Ppictures/ Shutterstock.com. Pg 32, Get Behind Trump girls, Dan Holm/Shutterstock.com. Pg 35, Big guns, Joseph Sohm/Shutterstock.com. Pg 36, Ghurkas, 1000 Words/ Shutterstock.com; Syrians sign. a katz/ Shutterstock.com. Pg 37, screaming girl, Tramvaen/Shutterstock.com. Pg 38, Cadillac, Betto Rodrigues/Shutterstock.com. Pg 39, musclemen, Christian De Araujo/Shutterstock.com; armored vehicles, Alexander Kuguchin/Shutterstock. com. Pg 40, tear-gassers, A_Lesik/Shutterstock.com. Pg 41, Trump, s_bukley/Shutterstock.com; Putin, Semen Lixodees/Shutterstock.com. Pg 45, Pres Clinton, stocklight/Shutterstock.com. Pg 46, Jeff Bezos, David Ryder/Getty Images; Bernie Madoff, Bloomberg/Getty Images. Pg 47, Ted Nugent, TDCPhotography/Shutterstock. com. Pg 48, Iron Man, REDXIII/ Shutterstock. com. Pg 49, Sarah Palin, mistydawnphoto/Shutterstock.com; Tiny Fey, Getty Images; Jeb Bush, Rich Koele/Shutterstock. com; Joe Lieberman, Joseph Sohm/Shutterstock.com; Mark Cuban, s_bukley/Shutterstock.com. Pg 50, Melania Trump, Everett Collection/Shutterstock.com. Pg 53, Trump hair, Albert H. Teich/Shutterstock.com. Pg 54, Versailles, Jose Ignacio Soto/Shutterstock.com. Pg 56, Mexican cuisine, Seamartini Graphics/Shutterstock.com /Shutterstock.com. Pg 60, fieldworkers, rightdx/Shutterstock.com.Page 61, Trump golfing, Getty Images; Pope, giulio napolitano/Shutterstock.com; foreign woman, OlegD/Shutterstock.com; refugees, Photoman29/Shutterstock.com. All other photos are from Shutterstock.com and istockphoto.com.